A VISIT TO

Germany

REVISED AND UPDATED

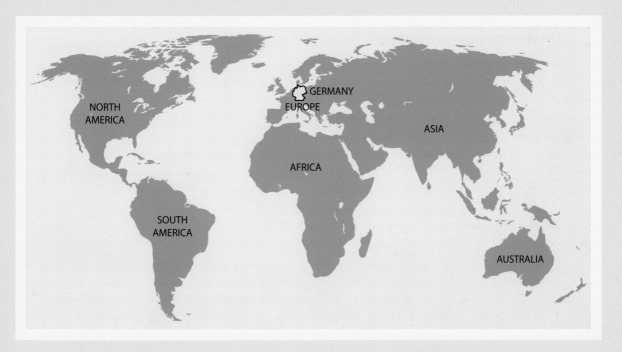

Rob Alcraft

Chicago, Illinois

Customer Service 888-454-2279

Visit our website at www.heinemannlibrary.com

Designed by Heinemann Library
Printed in China by South China Printing.

10 09 08
10 9 8 7 6 5 4 3 2 1

Library of Congress Cataloging-in-Publication Data
Alcraft, Rob, 1966-.
  Germany / by Rob Alcraft.
    p. cm. – (A visit to)
  Included bibliographical references and index.
  Summary: Introduces the land, landmarks, homes, food, clothing, work,
  transportation, language, and culture of Germany.
  ISBN: 978-1-4329-1267-3 (lib.bdg.); 978-1-4329-1286-4 (pbk)
    1. Germany—Pictorial works—Juvenile literature. I. Title. II. Title: Germany. III. Series.
DD17.A73
943—dc21

                                                99-18086

Acknowledgements
The publishers would like to thank the following for permission to reproduce photographs: ©AKG Photo p. 29; ©Corbis p. 14 (Zefa/Ted Levine); ©Getty Images p. 21 (Digital Vision/Jochen Sand), p. 25 (Westend61/ Michael Reusse); ©J Allan Cash pp. 10, 17, 19, 28; ©Photolibrary p. 12 (Fresh Food Images/Anthony Blake); ©Robert Harding Picture Library pp. 22, 27, p. 7 (G Hellier), p. 13 (Larsen-Collinge); ©Spectrum Colour Library p. 24; ©Telegraph Colour Library pp. 6, 27, pp. 5, 9, (Werner Otto), p. 8 (Bildarchiv Huber), pp. 11, 26 (David Norton), p. 15 (Josef Beck), p. 16 (Antonio Mo), p. 18 (Pfeiffer); ©Trip p. 20 (M O'Brien), p. 23 (M Barlow).

Cover photograph of monument near Europa Center, Berlin, Germany reproduced with permission of Robert Harding (Michael Jenner).

Our thanks to Nick Lapthorn and Clare Lewis in the preparation of this book.

Contents

Any words appearing in bold, **like this**, are explained in the Glossary.

Germany

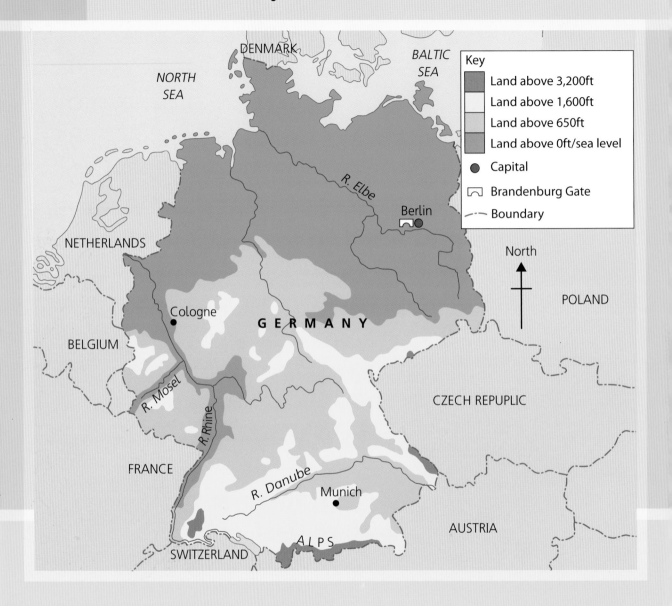

Germany is a big country. It is in the middle of Europe.

There are many big cities in Germany, like Berlin and Cologne (below). Most people in Germany live in cities.

There is a beautiful cathedral in the city of Cologne.

Land

In the north of Germany the land is flat and low. There are **marshes** and islands in the sea. Here the weather is wet and mild.

In the south of Germany are forests, **meadows** and mountains. The mountains are called the Alps. Winters here are very cold with lots of snow.

Summers in the Alps can be warm and sunny but there is still snow on the mountain tops.

Landmarks

Germany's biggest river is the Rhine. It is 820 miles long. Along the riverbanks are **vineyards** and beautiful castles.

The Brandenburg Gate is 200 years old.

This is the Brandenburg Gate. It stands in the middle of Berlin. Berlin is Germany's **capital** city.

Homes

Germany's towns and cities are crowded and busy. There is not much space for big houses and gardens. Many people live in apartments.

In the countryside there are old farmhouses. They have wide **sloping** roofs so the snow will slide off.

Farmhouses in the countryside are often built from wood.

Food

In Germany, lunch is an important meal. A popular meal is **schnitzel** with vegetables and mashed potatoes.

Sausage called wurst is a special German food. There are lots of different kinds of wurst. Some are eaten hot, and some are eaten cold. Some are sliced and some are **spicy**.

Clothes

Germans wear **modern** clothes, like jeans and T-shirts. In cold winters people have to wear thick coats and boots.

Clothing for festivals often have beautiful decorations.

At parties and festivals many Germans wear special clothes. They might wear leather shorts called lederhosen and a cap with feathers like this boy.

Work

Many Germans have jobs in factories, offices and shops. They make cars, trucks, machines and **electrical goods**.

Farmers use big machines like these to cut wheat.

In the country, farmers keep cows and pigs. They also grow grain, potatoes and fruit. The weather and soil are good for farming.

Transportation

There are many big **highways** in Germany. There are train stations in every city and busy airports.

Big ships carry coal, steel and oil along the rivers and canals.

On Germany's rivers and **canals** there are ships and **barges**. On the Rhine River ships from the sea can travel right into Germany.

Languages

In Germany people speak German. Some German and English words sound nearly the same, such as "buch" and "book," and "haus" and "house."

In German, there are two ways of speaking. You must use one way with adults and important people. The other way is for friends.

School

School starts early in Germany, at 7:30 AM. There is school on a Saturday, too. But lessons always finish at lunchtime, and everyone has the afternoon off.

These children are going on a school trip to the zoo.

When they are in class German children study many subjects, including math and German. They also have English lessons.

Free Time

Many Germans like going on holidays. In the summer, families often go to the beach. In winter when it snows, some people go skiing in the Alps.

Many Germans love sports. They join sports clubs, and play tennis and soccer. They go walking and camping in the forests and mountains.

Germans enjoy riding bikes, too.

Celebrations

Christmas is the most important celebration in Germany. There are special markets and fairs. The streets sparkle with lights.

Every year in July there is a children's festival. Children dress up in costumes and parade through the streets.

The Arts

Germany is famous for its beautiful music. Beethoven and Schumann were German. They wrote music for **orchestras** and for the piano.

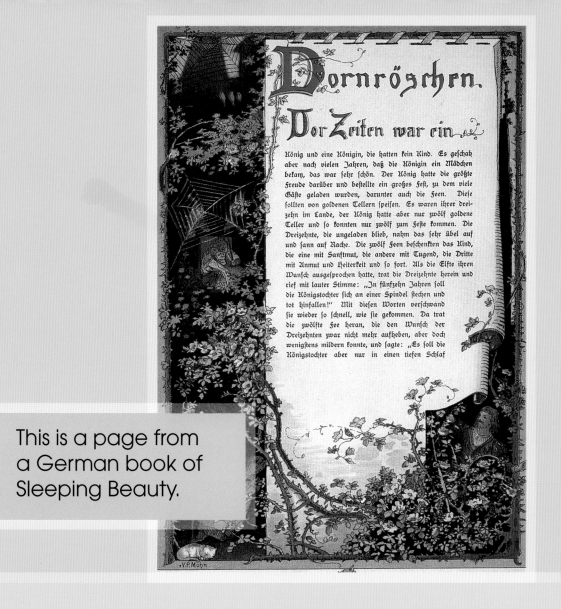

This is a page from a German book of Sleeping Beauty.

Have you heard the story of Sleeping Beauty? This is a very old German **fairy tale**, written down by two brothers called Grimm.

Factfile

Name	The Federal Republic of Germany
Capital	Germany's **capital** city is called Berlin.
Language	German
Population	There are 82 million people living in Germany.
Money	German money is called the euro.
Religions	Most Germans are Christians but there are many other religions, too.
Products	Germany makes chemicals, cars and trucks, machines and **electrical goods**.

Words You Can Learn

guten tag (goo-ten targ)	hello
auf wiedersehen (owf vee-d-say-n)	goodbye
ja (ya)	yes
nein (nine)	no
danke schön (danke shern)	thank you
bitte (bitter)	please
eins (eye-n)	one
zwei (svi)	two
drei (dry)	three

Glossary

barge a boat with a flat bottom. It can float in shallow water.

canal a river dug by people

capital the city where the government is based

electrical goods things like televisions and video recorders which use electricity

fairy tale a story where anything can happen

marshes flat, wet places

meadow grassy land

modern new, up-to-date

orchestra a group of people who play music

schnitzel fried meat in breadcrumbs

sloping leaning

spicy food with a strong, hot taste

vineyard place where grapes are grown

Index